UNISON/TWO-PART TREBLE VOICES

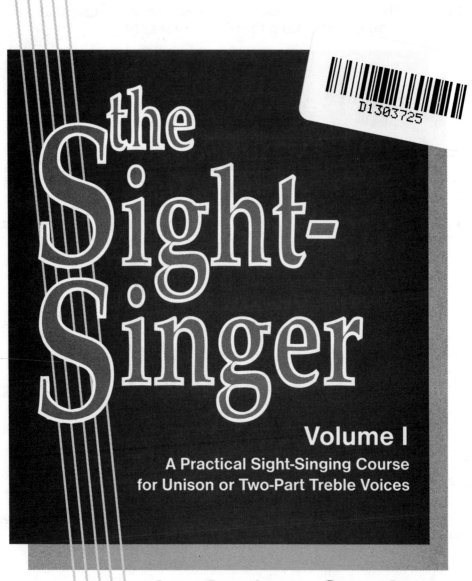

the
Sight-
Singer

Volume I
A Practical Sight-Singing Course
for Unison or Two-Part Treble Voices

by Audrey Snyder

THE BEAT AND THE RHYTHM

In music the *beat* is the pulse which underlies the music that is heard. In most music it is important to keep the beat very steady.

Rhythm may move either *with* the beat, *faster* than the beat or *slower* than the beat.

Play the beat and speak these rhythms:

1.

The speed with which the beat moves is called the *tempo*. Do these next exercises first at a slow tempo and then at a faster tempo.

Play the beat and speak these rhythms:

MORE RHYTHM

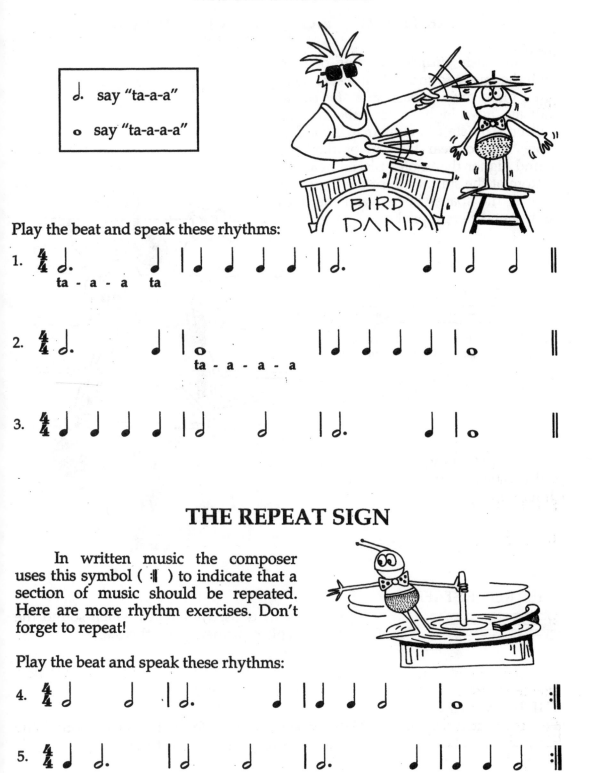

| ♩. | say "ta-a-a" |
| o | say "ta-a-a-a" |

Play the beat and speak these rhythms:

1. (rhythm exercise)
   ta - a - a   ta

2. (rhythm exercise)
   ta - a - a - a

3. (rhythm exercise)

THE REPEAT SIGN

In written music the composer uses this symbol (:||) to indicate that a section of music should be repeated. Here are more rhythm exercises. Don't forget to repeat!

Play the beat and speak these rhythms:

4. (rhythm exercise)

5. (rhythm exercise)

6. (rhythm exercise)

PITCH

TREBLE STAFF,   BASS STAFF,   GRAND STAFF

In music *pitch* is how low or how high the music sounds. Composers most often place music notes on a *staff* ▤ to indicate how high or low the sounds will be. The staff is similar to a ladder. Notes placed near the top of the staff sound higher than notes placed near the bottom of the staff. Each of the lines and each of the spaces in between the lines represent different pitches.

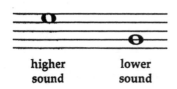

| higher | lower |
| sound | sound |

In written music, staffs (sometimes called staves) are labeled in several different ways.

THE TREBLE STAFF

The *treble* staff is used for notes which sound the highest. Higher voices primarily use this staff.

THE BASS STAFF

The *bass* staff is used for notes which sound the lowest. Lower voices primarily use this staff.

When the treble staff and the bass staff are *joined together*, they become what is called the *grand* staff.

THE GRAND STAFF

Treble Staff for higher voices

Bass Staff for lower voices

Middle C

The note in the middle is called Middle C. It joins the treble and bass staffs together. The short, little line which cuts through the center of Middle C is called a *ledger line*.

In this course we will use only the notes found on the treble staff, since the notes on the treble staff are the most comfortable for higher voices to sing.

PITCH

DO, RE and MI

As you know, when a note head (• or ◦) is placed on the treble staff it represents a sound called a *pitch*, which can be:

higher    or lower    or somewhere in the middle

It is the note *head* (• or ◦) which represents the pitch. The *stem* of the note may go either up or down without affecting the pitch or the rhythm.

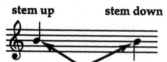

The note *head* is in the same place, so the pitch is the same.

In quite a lot of choral music, *DO* is the pitch which represents the *home base*. It is often the pitch center to which all other pitches relate.

1.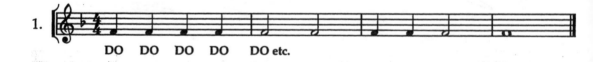

DO   DO   DO   DO   DO etc.

2.

DO

Re is known by its *relationship to DO*. It is always the upper next-door neighbor to DO.

DO   Re

3.

DO DO DO DO   Re

4.

DO   Re   DO

Mi is known by its *relationship to DO and Re*. Mi is always the upper next-door neighbor to Re.

DO   Re   Mi

5.

DO   Re   Mi   Re

6.

DO

FASTER RHYTHM

Some music notes move more quickly than others.

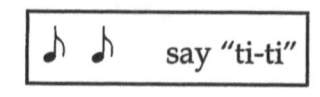

say "ti-ti"

1.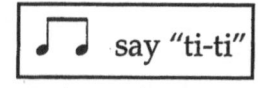

ta   ta   ta   ta   ta   ti-ti

Another way to write ♪♪ is ♫. The composer removes the flags (♩) and puts a beam across the stem of the two notes, like this:

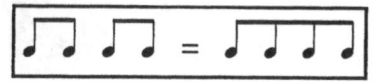

say "ti-ti"

2.

ta   ta   ta   ta   ti-ti

Often in written music, when two or more ♫s are in a row, the composer will simply connect the beam on the top, like this:

3.

ti - ti - ti - ti

4.

DO

5.

DO

REVIEW AND PRACTICE

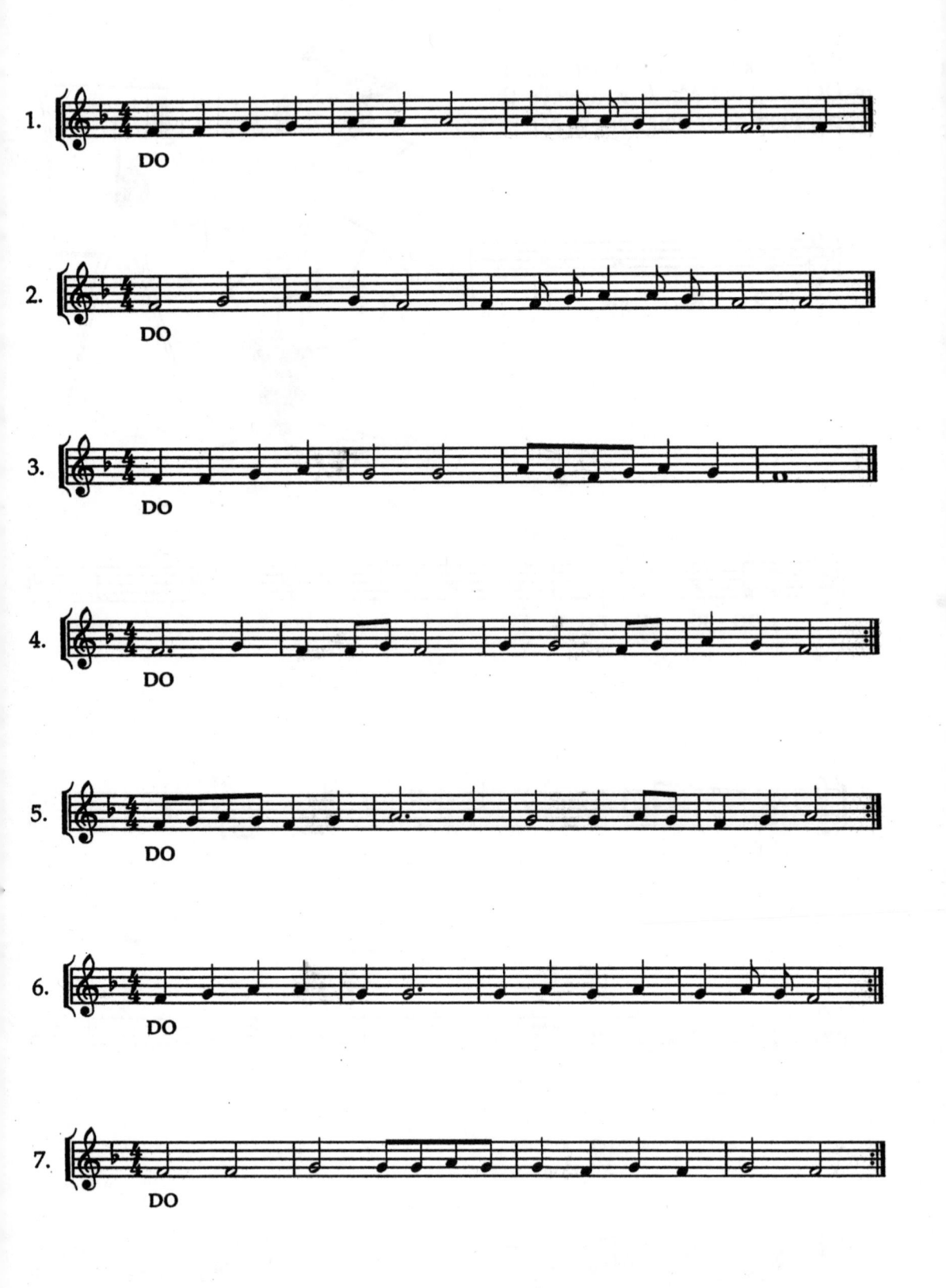

ADD FA AND SOL

Fa is known by its *relationship* to *DO, Re, and Mi.* It is always the upper next-door neighbor to *Mi.*

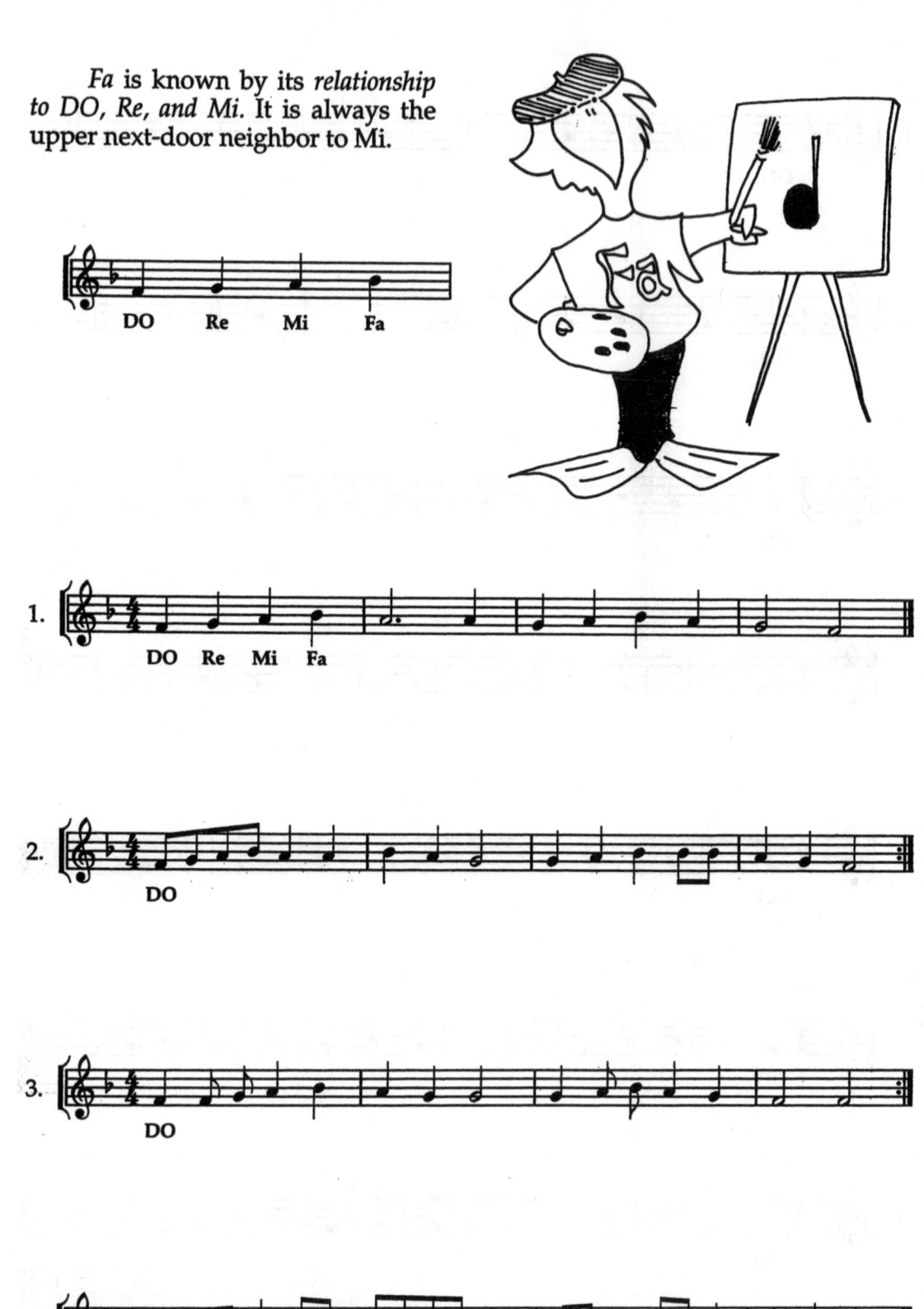

Sol is known by its *relationship to DO, Re, Mi, and Fa.* Sol is always the upper next-door neighbor to Fa.

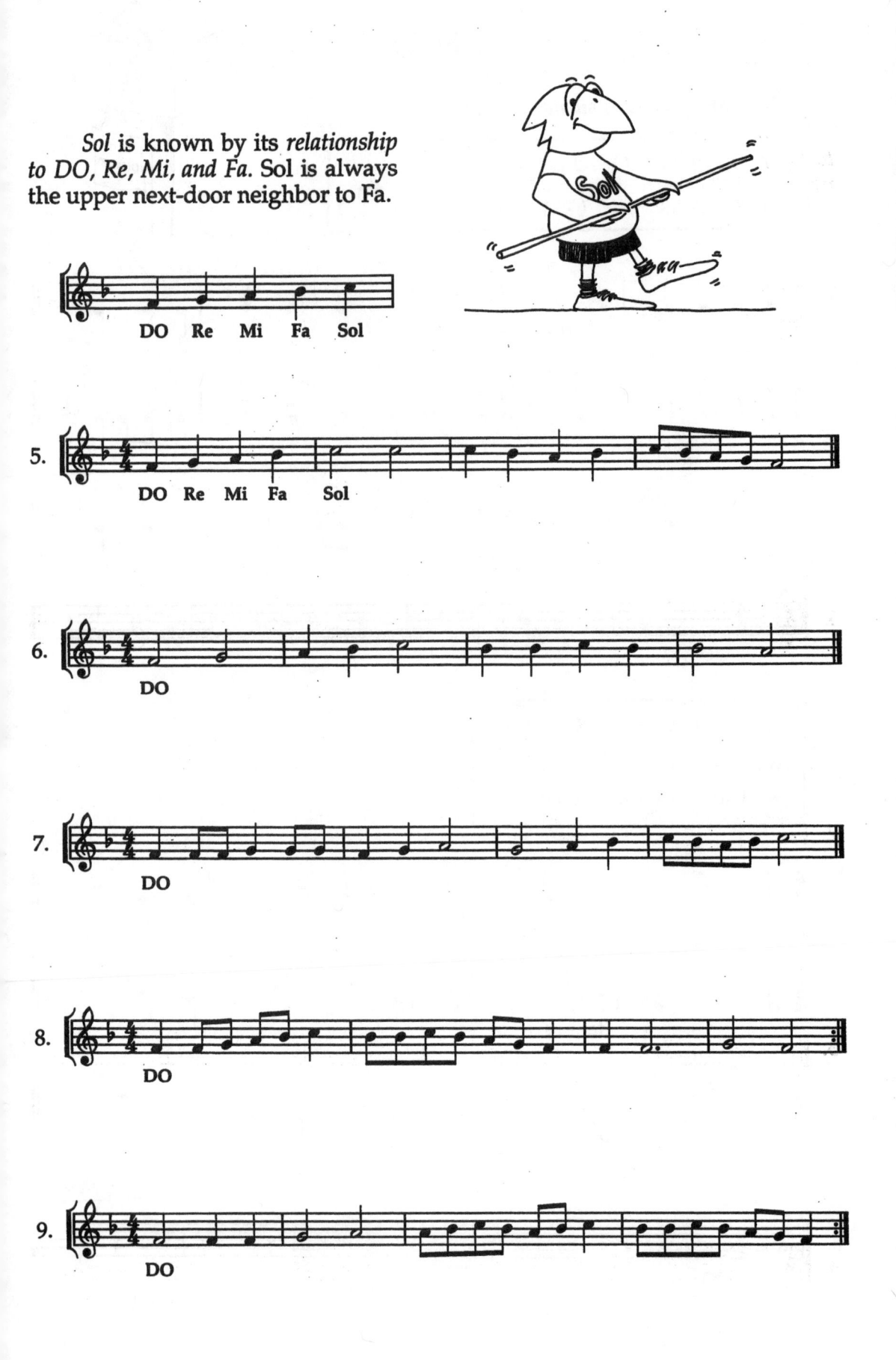

DO   Re   Mi   Fa   Sol

5.

DO   Re   Mi   Fa   Sol

6.

DO

7.

DO

8.

DO

9.

DO

RESTS

Rests are places of *silence* in music.

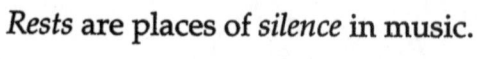

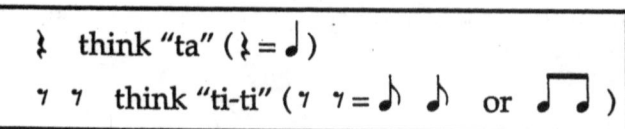

1. (ta)

2. (ti-ti)

3.

4. DO

> ■ think "ta-a" (■ = ♩)
> ■. think "ta-a-a" (■. = ♩.)
> ▬ think "ta-a-a-a" (▬ = o)

5. (ta - a)

6. (ta - a - a)

7. (ta - a - a - a)

8. DO

SIGHT-SINGING IN PARTS

When writing choral music, composers use a bracket { at the left side of the page. To show that more than one voice part will sing together at the same time, the composer will enlarge the bracket to include as many staffs (staves) as needed.

MEASURES

Barlines (|) are used by composers to *group* music notes and rests together. The area between two barlines is called a *measure*.

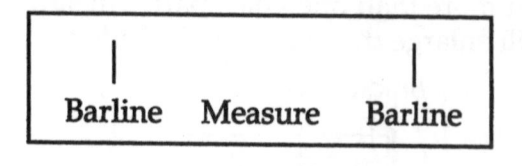

Barline   Measure   Barline

When writing music composers decide the number of beats which will be put in each measure. Any number of beats can be put in a measure, but the most common are 2, 3, 4 and 6. Until now, all of the exercises in this course have had 4 beats per measure. Using ♩ as the beat, here are some exercises with 3 beats per measure.

Exercises with 2 beats per measure:

Exercises with 6 beats per measure:

7.

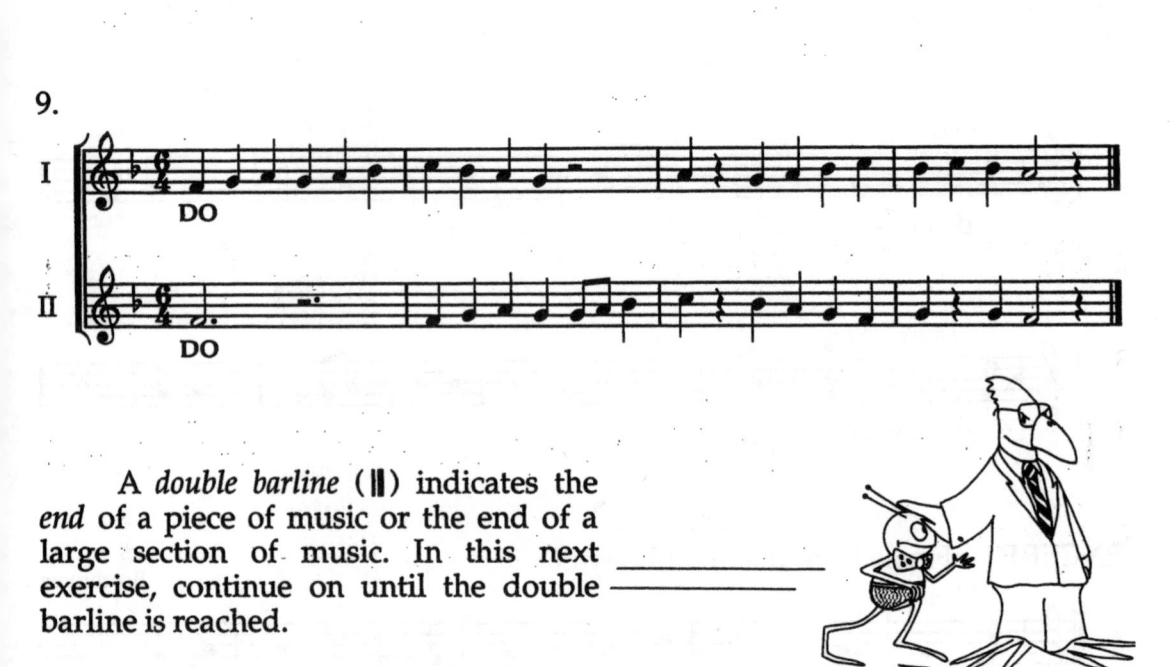

8. DO

9.

I DO

II DO

A *double barline* (‖) indicates the *end* of a piece of music or the end of a large section of music. In this next exercise, continue on until the double barline is reached.

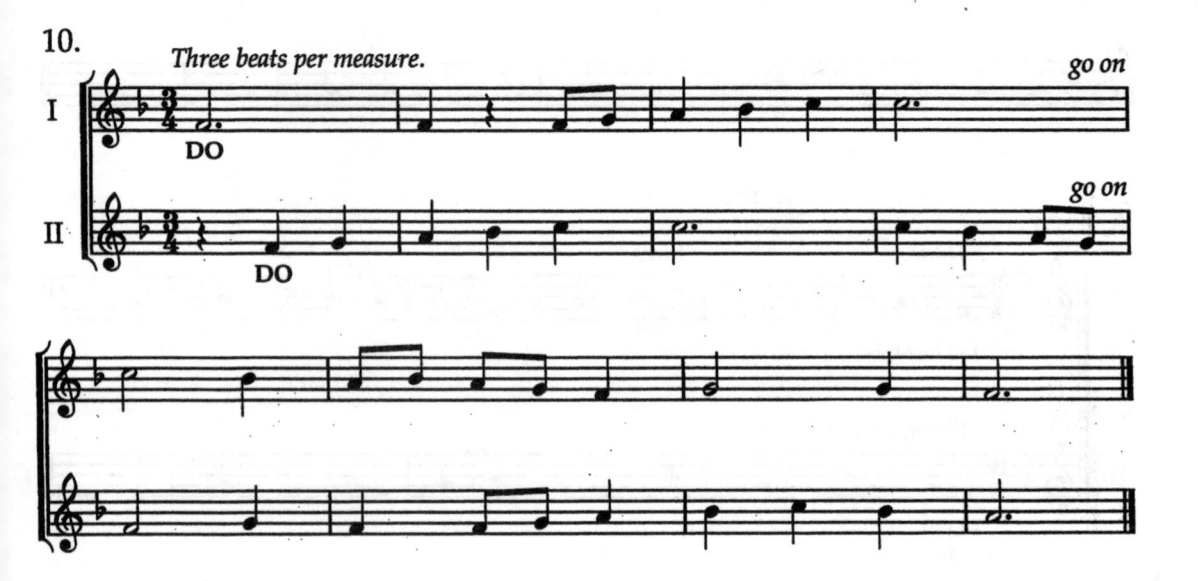

10.

Three beats per measure.   *go on*

I DO

   go on

II DO

MUSIC BEGINS ON DIFFERENT PITCHES

Music does not *always* begin on DO. Music can begin on *any* pitch.

DO CAN MOVE

When a composer chooses to write music on a staff, he or she will decide where DO should be placed. This decision is usually based on how high or low the composer wants the music to sound and also on which notes most voices can sing comfortably and well. *DO can be placed anywhere on the staff.*

As you know, DO can be here:

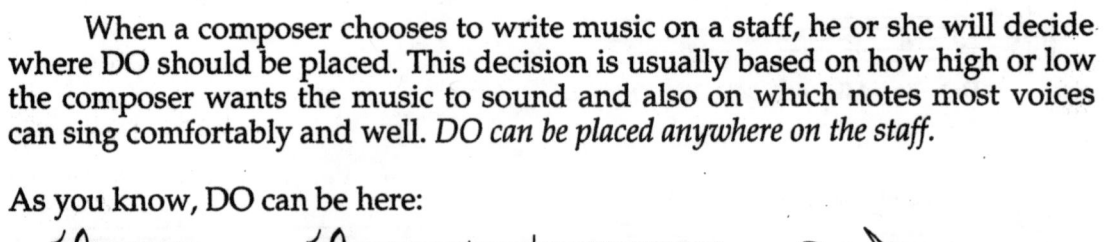

or DO can be here:

Remember that Re, Mi, Fa, and Sol are known by their *relationship* to each other as next-door neighbors. No matter if they fall on a line or in a space, they follow the same next-door neighbor pattern.

DO can be here:

or DO can be here:

Each person's voice is unique. For every individual singer, some pitches will be comfortable to sing without straining and others will not be comfortable to sing. Every person's voice will change throughout his or her lifetime. Pitches which may be easy to sing today may be more difficult to sing in a few months or years from now. The opposite is also true. Pitches which may be impossible to sing today may be easy to sing in a few months or years from now.

18

LETTER NAMES ON THE STAFF

Each line and each space on the staff has an alphabet letter name. Alphabet letter names proceed from A through G. Then the pattern of A through G repeats again and again.

Grand Staff

D E F G A B C D E F...

...G A B C D E F G A B C

Every excellent sight-singer eventually memorizes the letter names of the lines and spaces. Here are some patterns which may help in the memorization process:

Space notes

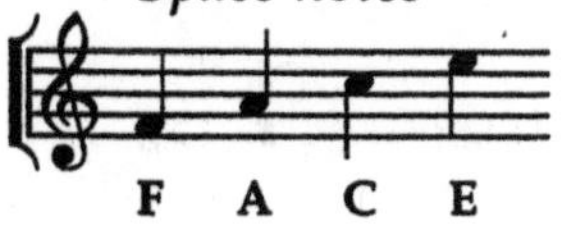

Spell FACE

F A C E

Line notes

Every Good Boy Deserves Fudge

E G B D F

As you know, DO can be placed anywhere on the staff. In quite a lot of choral music DO represents the home base. It is often the pitch center to which all of the other pitches relate.

The *pitch center* or *home base* is also called the *KEY*.

If a composer decides that the pitch center (DO) should be placed where G is on the staff, then that piece of music is said to be in the key of G Major.

If the pitch center (DO) is F, then the piece of music is in the key of F Major.

1. Key of F Major

2. Key of E Major

MORE LEDGER LINES

Sometimes composers want to write notes which sound higher or lower than those on the staff. As you know, music staffs are somewhat like ladders. Composers use short, little lines called *ledger lines* to create extra lines and spaces for these notes. (It is similar to adding an extension on a ladder.)

Ledger lines look like this:

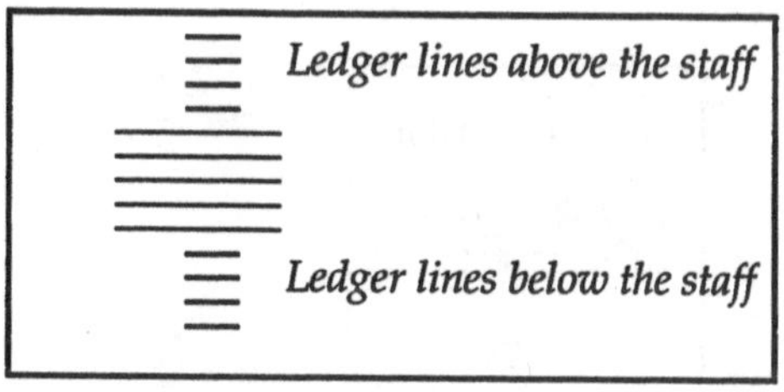

Ledger lines above the staff

Ledger lines below the staff

Ledger line notes *below* the treble staff:

C   B   A

Ledger line notes *above* the treble staff:

A   B   C

1. Key of A Major
Think and sing

DO

2. Key of A Major
Think and sing

DO

3. Key of B Major
Think and sing

DO

*Cue notes are optional notes if range is too low.

TEMPO CHANGES
RITARDANDO, FERMATA AND ACCELERANDO

As you know, the *speed* at which the beat moves is called the *tempo*. To indicate that the music should become *gradually slower*, composers use the word *ritardando*. It is often abbreviated in written music and appears as *ritard.* or *rit.*

When a composer wants a note to be *held longer* than its usual length, he or she will place this symbol ⌢ , called a *fermata*, above the note.

Composers use *accel.* (which is an abbreviation for *accelerando*) to indicate that the music should become *gradually faster*.

REVIEW AND PRACTICE

1. Key of G Major

2. Key of F Major

Think, Sing

3. Key of E Major

4. Key of F Major

5. Key of G Major

6. Key of F Major

7. Key of B Major

SKIPS
DO - MI - SOL

As you know, the staff is like a ladder, where notes step up and step down using the lines and spaces. Music does not *always* move only in steps. Sometimes music moves in *skips*.

Steps, lines and spaces
Key of G Major

DO Re Mi Fa Sol Fa Mi Re DO

Skips, line to line
Key of G Major

DO Mi Sol Mi DO

Skips, space to space
Key of F Major

DO Mi Sol Mi DO

1. Key of G Major

DO Mi Sol

MYSTERY TUNE

2. Key of F Major

Think, Sing

DO Re Mi

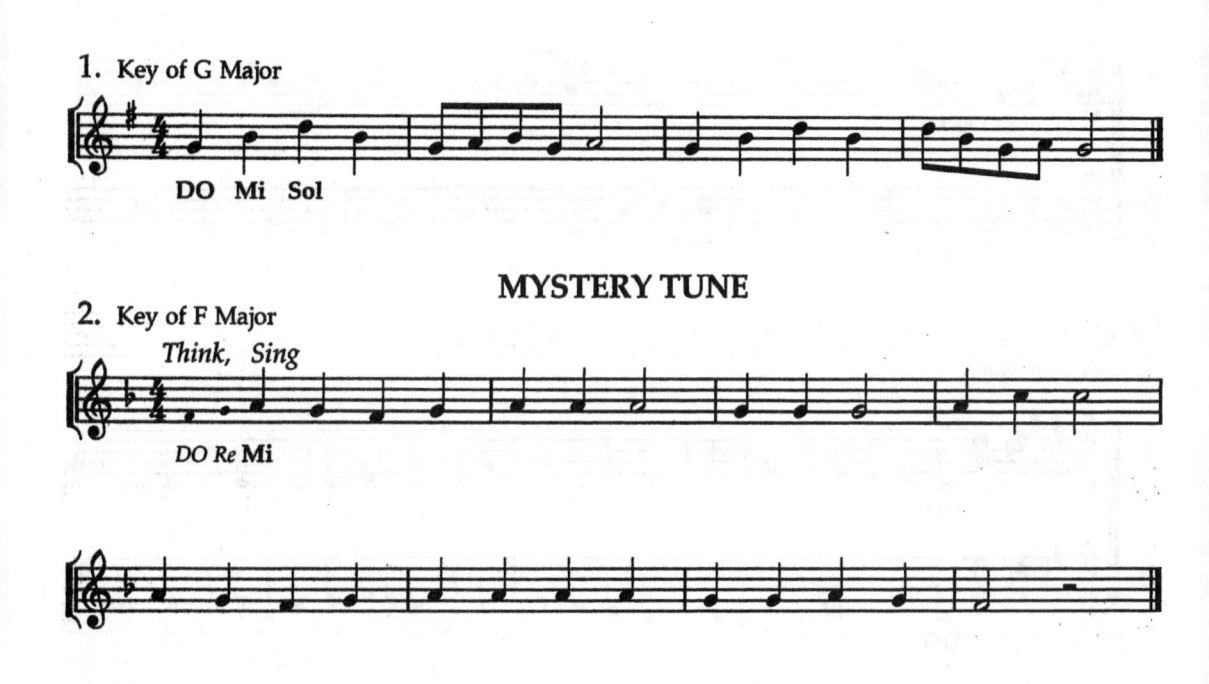

MORE SKIPS
RE - FA - RE

1. Key of E Major

AUNT RHODY: EXCERPT

2. Key of G Major

3. Key of F Major

LIGHTLY ROW

4. Key of G Major

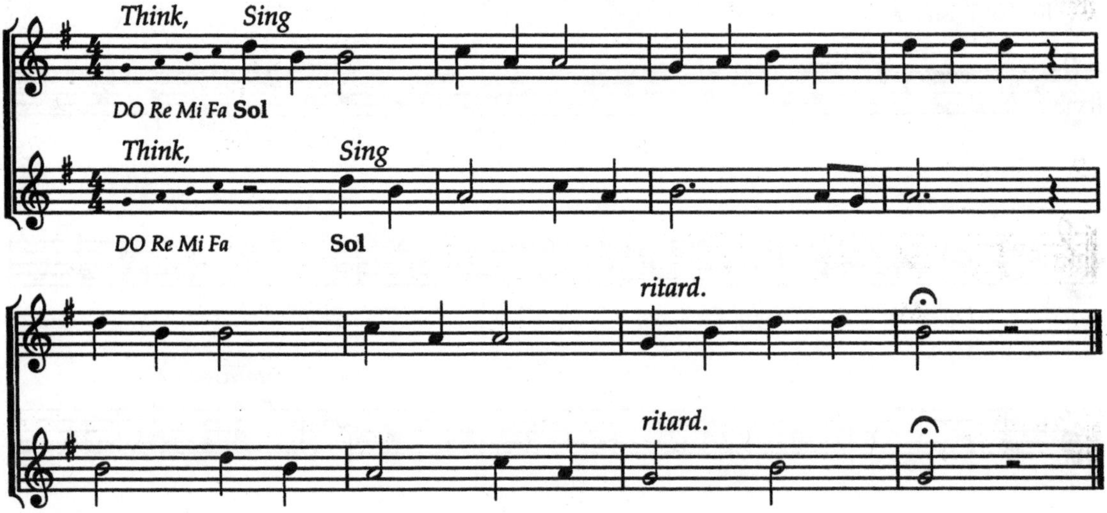

METER SIGNATURE:
BEATS PER MEASURE

At the beginning of a piece of music, near the left side of the staff, the composer will place two numbers, one above the other, such as $\frac{3}{4}$. This is called a *meter signature* or *time signature*. In music, unlike in mathematics, these numbers do *not* indicate a fraction. Each of these numbers has its own separate meaning. The significance of the bottom number will be explained later in the course. *The top number tells the singer how many beats there will be in each measure.*

How many beats per measure do each of these indicate?

A. $\frac{3}{4}$ B. $\frac{4}{4}$ C. $\frac{6}{4}$

D. $\frac{2}{4}$ E. $\frac{6}{8}$

Sometimes the composer will change the number of beats per measure in the middle of a piece.

1. Key of F Major

ADD LA

La is known by its *relationship to DO, Re, Mi, Fa and Sol*. La is always the upper next-door neighbor to Sol.

Key of F Major

DO Re Mi Fa Sol La

Step up to La:

1. Key of F Major **LONG, LONG AGO**

DO Sol La Sol

ritard.

2. Key of F Major

DO

Skip up to La:

3. Key of E Major

DO Fa La Sol

4. Key of C Major

DO Fa La Sol

ADD TI

    Ti is known by its *relationship to DO, Re, Mi, Fa, Sol and La.* Ti is always the upper next-door neighbor to La.

Key of E Major

DO Re Mi Fa Sol La Ti

Step up to Ti:

1. Key of E Major

DO   La Ti La

2. Key of C Major

DO

Skip up to Ti:

3. Key of D Major

Think, Sing

DO *Re* Mi Fa Sol Ti   La

4. Key of C Major

Think,   *Sing*

I

DO *Re Mi Fa* **Sol**

Think,   *Sing*

II

DO *Re*   **Mi**

ADD HIGH DO

High DO is known by its *relationship to low DO, Re, Mi, Fa, Sol, La and Ti.* Like low DO, high DO acts as a home base too. It is always the upper next-door neighbor to Ti:

Key of D Major

DO Re Mi Fa Sol La Ti DO

Step up to High DO:

1. Key of D Major

Think, *Sing*

DO Re Mi Fa **Sol** **La** **Ti** **DO**

2. Key of B Major

Think, *Sing*

DO Re Mi Fa **Sol**

Skip up to High DO:

3. Key of C Major

Think, *Sing*

DO Re Mi Fa **Sol** **La** **DO** **Ti**

Step up to High DO:

4. Key of B Major

I

DO

Think, *Sing*

II

DO Re Mi Fa **Sol**

Congratulations! You have learned *all* of the notes which make up the *pattern* called the *Major Scale* (DO Re Mi Fa Sol La Ti DO). Since a lot of music written in the past and a lot of music composed today uses the Major Scale pattern, you have taken a big step in becoming a self-sufficient sight-singer!

REVIEW AND PRACTICE

1. Key of C Major

DO Sol

2. Key of B Major

DO Mi

3. Key of C Major

DO Mi

DO Mi

LET MUSIC LIVE

MORE RHYTHM

♪ and 𝄾

Review:
♫ say "ti-ti"
♪ ♪ say "ti-ti"
𝄾 𝄾 think "ti-ti"

New rhythm:
♪ say "ti"
𝄾 think "ti"

1. (rhythm line) ti (ti)

2. (rhythm line)

3. (rhythm line)

4. Key of G Major

DO

5. Key of C Major

I ... DO Mi

II ... DO

TIES

A tie is a curved line which composers use to connect or "tie" together notes which are the *same pitch*. To count notes which are tied together, drop the "T" from the second note.

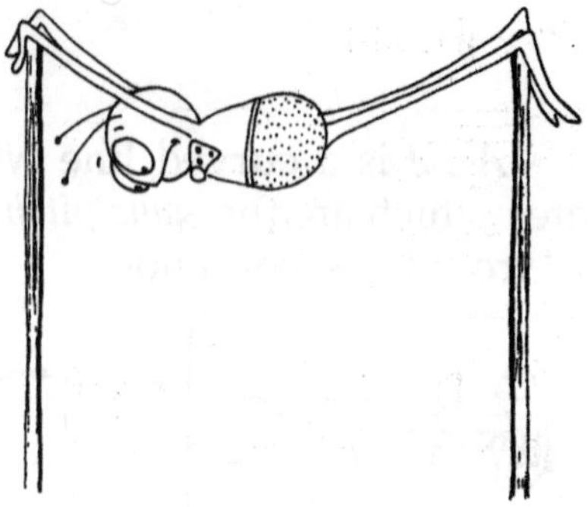

say "ta - i - ti"

1.  ta - i - ti

2.

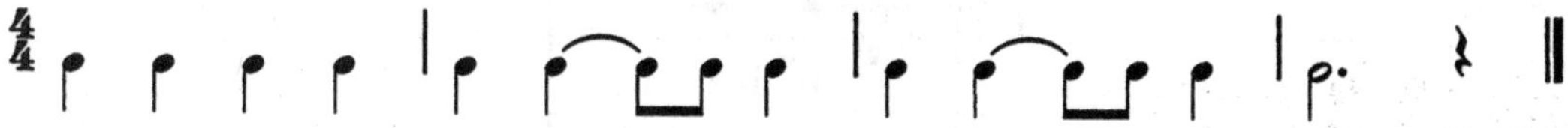

There is another way in which   can be written. Composers will sometimes use a dotted note instead, like this:

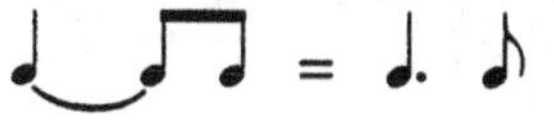

say "ta - i - ti"   "ta-i-ti"

3.  ta - i - ti

EXCERPT from THE NEW WORLD SYMPHONY

4. Key of F Major

Dvořák

DO Mi   Sol

1. Key of C Major

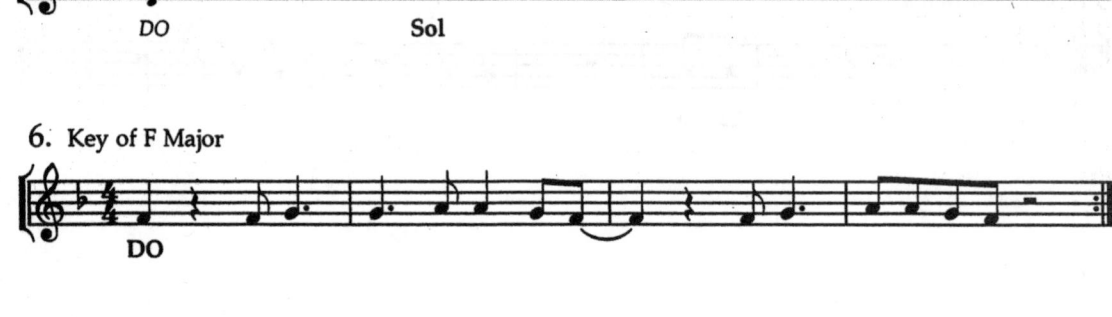

DO Mi   Fa   Sol

There is another way in which  (ti-ti-a) can be written. Composers will sometimes use a dotted note for this too.

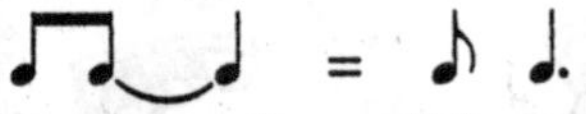

say "ti - ti - a" say "ti - ta-i"
("syn-co")

2. ti - ta - i   ta   ta
(syn-co)

3. Key of G Major

DO

ti - ta - i
(syn-co)

4. Key of G Major

DO Mi

5. Key of D Major

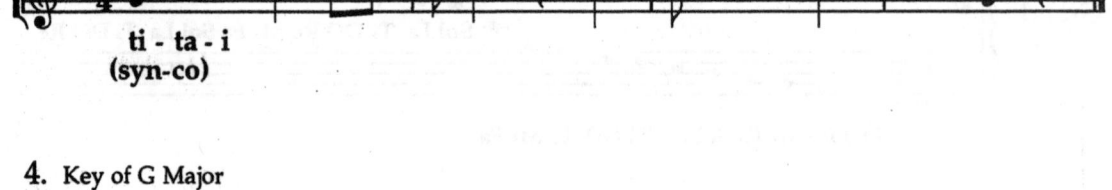

DO Sol

DO   Sol

6. Key of F Major

DO

DOWN FROM DO

As you know, music notes can go from the lower DO on up to the higher DO. Music notes can go *down* the staff from lower DO too.

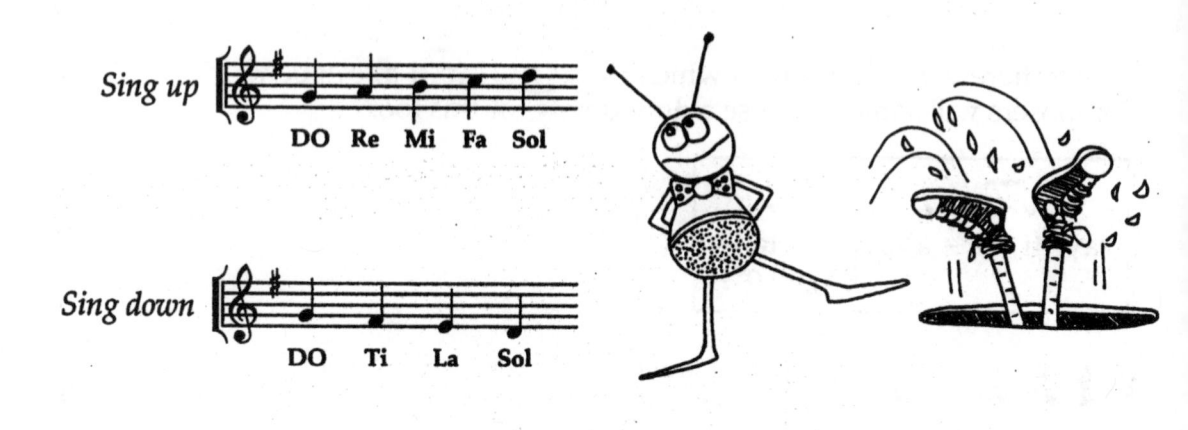

Sing up   DO Re Mi Fa Sol

Sing down   DO Ti La Sol

In music, regardless of how high or low the notes go, the Major scale *pattern* remains the *same.*

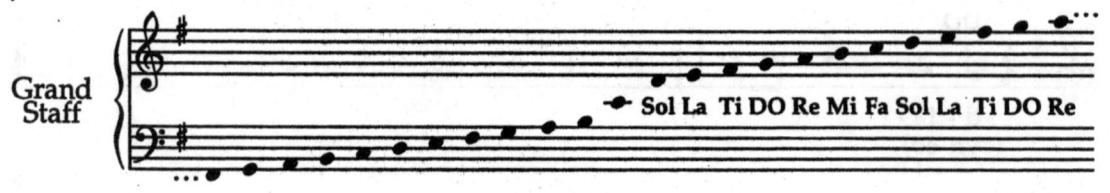

Grand Staff

Sol La Ti DO Re Mi Fa Sol La Ti DO Re

Ti DO Re Mi Fa Sol La Ti DO Re Mi Fa

HOLIDAY MYSTERY TUNE EXCERPT

1. Key of F Major

DO Sol   DO Ti DO

2. Key of C Major

DO   Ti Ti   La La Sol

MORE RHYTHM

RHYTHM REVIEW AND PRACTICE

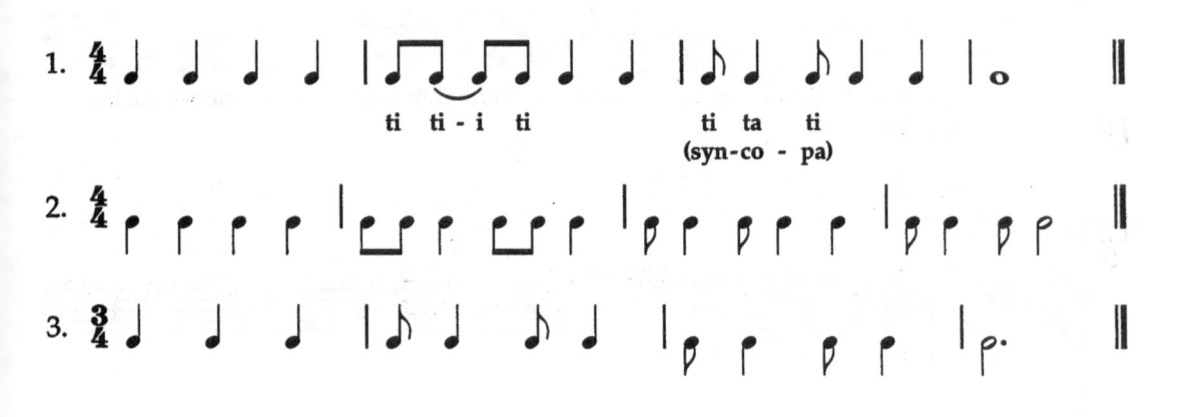

REVIEW AND PRACTICE

ALL THROUGH THE NIGHT EXCERPT

1. Key of B Major

Sleep   my child, let   peace at-tend thee   all   through the   night.

WE WANT THE CHANCE

Audrey Snyder

2. Key of D Major

We want the chance to be____ all we can be,____ the chance to be   all we can be!

We want the chance to be____ all we can be,____ the chance to be   all we can be!

3. Key of F Major

4. Key of E Major

MORE SKIPS
TI - RE - TI

Key of C Major

DO Re Mi Fa Sol La Ti DO Re DO Ti La Sol Fa Mi Re DO

Ti Re Ti DO

1. Key of C Major

DO   Ti Re DO

2. Key of B Major

DO Ti

3. Key of A Major

I   DO

II   *DO* Sol

PATRIOTIC MYSTERY TUNE EXCERPT

4. Key of G Major

I   *melody*   *ritard.*

DO

II   *ritard.*

DO Mi

REVIEW AND PRACTICE

1. Key of E Major

MAKE THE WORLD A BETTER PLACE

Audrey Snyder

DO

I

Give a lit-tle smile to your neigh-bor, Show a lit-tle care to - day,____

DO

II

Give a lit-tle smile to your neigh-bor, Show a lit-tle care to - day,____

Share a lit-tle laugh-ter and hap-pi-ness, Make the world a bet-ter place._

Share a lit-tle laugh-ter and hap-pi-ness, Make the world a bet-ter place._

2. Key of A Major

rit.

I

DO   Sol

rit.

II

DO

3. Key of D Major

DO Sol

DYNAMICS

As you know, music can sound high and low and can move fast and slowly. Music can also be *loud* and *soft*. The *degree* of loudness and softness in music is called *dynamics*. Composers use symbols to tell performers how loudly and softly they would like the music to be performed. In choral music the most commonly used symbols are:

ppp	=	very, very soft *(pianississimo)*
pp	=	very soft *(pianissimo)*
p	=	soft *(piano)*
m p	=	medium soft *(mezzo-piano)*
mf	=	medium loud *(mezzo-forte)*
f	=	loud *(forte)*
ff	=	very loud *(fortissimo)*
fff	=	very, very loud *(fortissississimo)*
cresc.	=	gradually become louder *(crescendo)*
decresc.	=	gradually become softer *(decrescendo)*
sfz	=	suddenly strikingly loud *(sforzando)*
sub. p	=	suddenly very soft *(subito piano)*

FOG

Audrey Snyder

1. Key of G Major

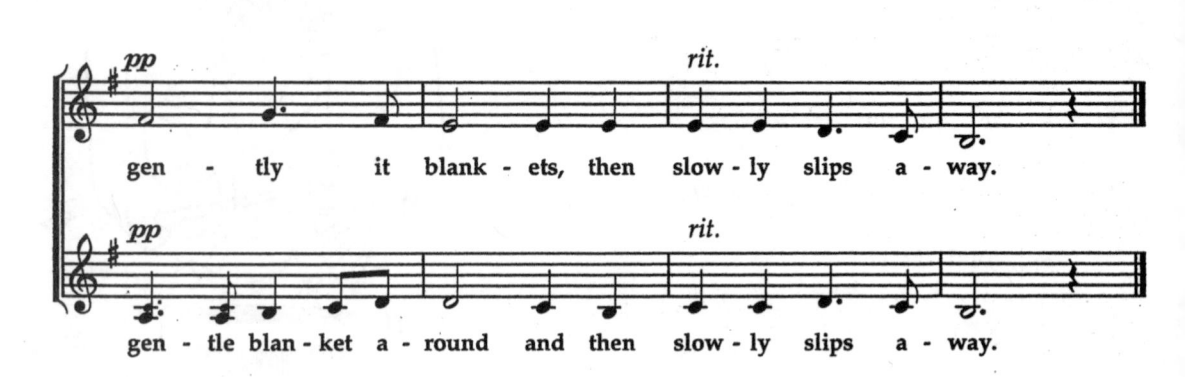

A SMILE

Audrey Snyder

2. Key of D Major

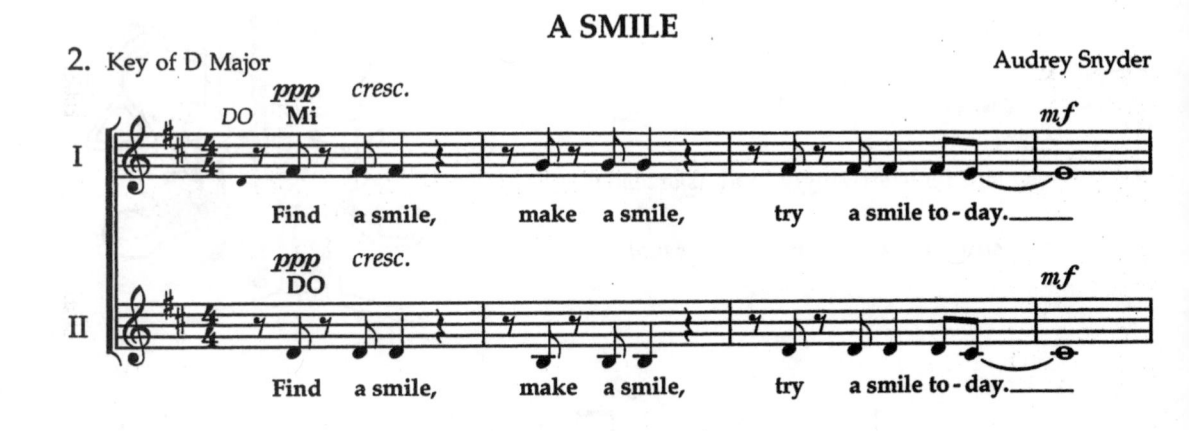

JUMPS
JUMPING DO - SOL - DO

As you know, music moves in steps and skips. Music also moves in *jumps*. Jumps occur when two notes are *farther apart than a skip*.

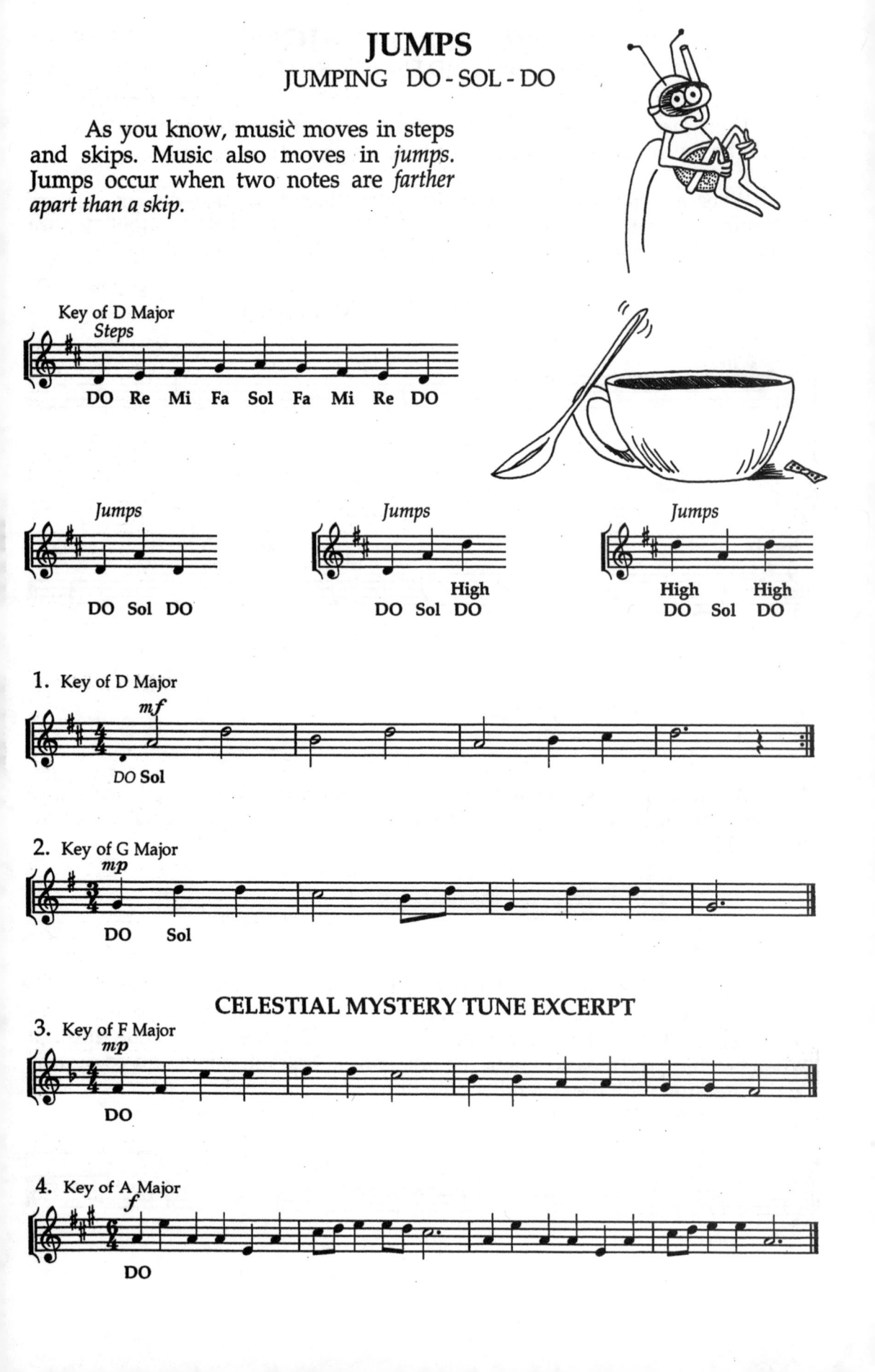

MUSICAL ROADSIGNS
FIRST AND SECOND ENDINGS, D.C., D.S., ‖:

There are many ways in which composers indicate that sections of music should be repeated. As you know, the repeat sign (:‖) is one way.

When a composer wants a section of music to be repeated from the very beginning, he or she will sometimes write *D.C.* which is the abbreviation for *Da Capo*, which in Italian means "The Head."

STILL IN BED? MYSTERY ROUND

1. Key of E Major

When a composer wants a section of music to be repeated but to *end differently* the second time, he or she will use brackets and numbers to indicate it, like this:

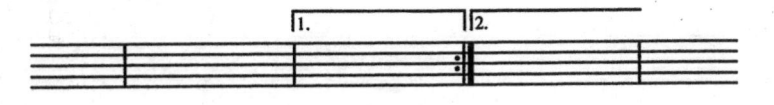

These brackets are placed above certain measures of music to indicate the *first ending* and the *second ending*. Sing from the beginning of the music to the repeat sign. Then go back and repeat the music. On this second time through, when reaching the measure with the first ending bracket, skip it and go directly to the measure with the second ending bracket without missing a beat.

2. Key of G Major

When a composer wants a section of music to be repeated not from the beginning, but from *another* place in the music, he or she will write *D.S.* and place a sign (𝄋) in the music to mark the place where the repeated section should begin. D.S. is an abbreviation for *Dal Segno*, which in Italian means "The Sign."

FOLK SONG

1. Key of E Major

Flemish

mf

DO Mi

Another way in which composers indicate repeated sections is to use repeat signs that are turned around the other way (𝄆). This sign (𝄆) indicates the place where the repeated section begins.

PEOPLE OF THE WORLD

2. Key of C Major

Audrey Snyder

I

DO   *mp* Sol

Wheth-er   black or white   or yel - low   or brown, a

II

DO   *mp* Sol

Wheth-er   black or white   or yel - low   or brown, a

sis - ter   or broth - er, the   peo - ple of   the world   need to learn how to

sis - ter   or broth - er, the   peo - ple of   the world   need to learn how to

live with re - spect   for one an - oth - er, wheth-er   oth - er.

live with re - spect   for one an - oth - er, wheth-er   oth - er.

REVIEW AND PRACTICE

1. Key of F Major

CANINE MYSTERY TUNE

2. Key of A Major

MIRRORS

3. Key of F Major

STACCATO AND LEGATO

A composer will put a *dot* above or below a note to indicate that it should be sung or played short. The dot is called a *staccato* mark.

1. Key of F Major

When a composer wants notes to be played or sung very *smoothly* and *connected* with no space in between, he or she will write the word *legato*.

2. Key of G Major

SLUR

Another way in which composers will indicate connected, smooth singing or playing is with the use of a *slur*. A slur is a curved line that connects notes which are *different in pitch*. (A slur and a tie look very similar. The difference is that a tie connects together notes of the *same* pitch, and a slur connects together notes of *different* pitches.) In choral music, slurs are used when more than one note is sung on one syllable of text.

3. Key of A Major

STACCATO MARCH

4. Key of C Major

REVIEW AND PRACTICE

SWEET BETSY

1. Key of C Major

American Folk Song

Legato **mf** DO

I

Oh, do you re - mem - ber Sweet Bet - sy from

mf DO

II

Oh, do you re - mem - ber Sweet Bet - sy from

Pike? She crossed the wide prair - ie with her hus - band

mp

Pike? She crossed the prair - ie with her hus - band

Ike, with two yoke of ox - en and a big yal - ler

mf

Ike, Ah

mf *rit.*

dog, a tall Shang-hai roos - ter and one spot - ted hog.

mp *rit.*

— a tall roos - ter, one spot - ted hog.

SEE, THE CONQUERING HERO COMES

2. Key of D Major

Handel

f

DO **Sol**

AULD LANG SYNE EXCERPT

1. Key of E Major   Scottish

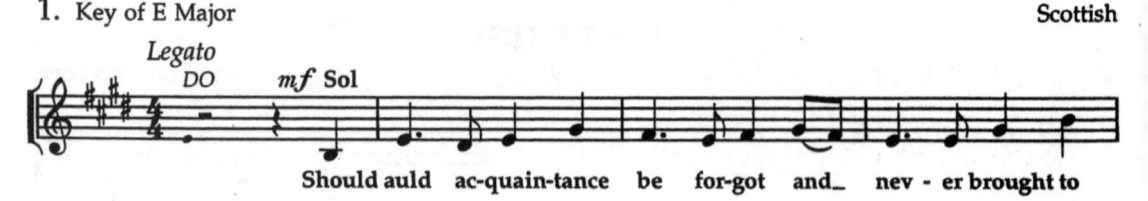

Legato

Should auld ac-quain-tance be for-got and_ nev - er brought to

mind? Should auld ac-quain-tance be for-got and_ days of auld lang syne?

Notice that AULD LANG SYNE begins with three beats of rests. To simplify the appearance, composers will sometimes omit the beginning rests in the first measure of the piece. The remaining note (or notes) is called a *pickup note*.

THE ASH GROVE EXCERPT

2. Key of G Major   English

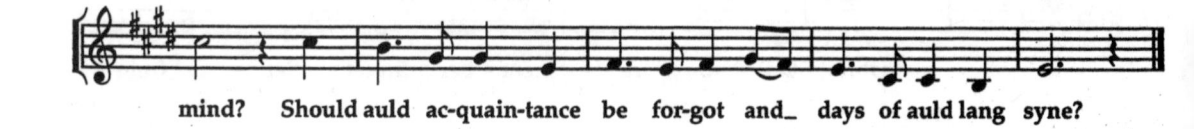

Legato

From yon - der green_ val - ley where stream - lets_ me -

From yon - der val - ley, stream - lets_ me -

an - der, where twi - light_ is_ fad - ing, I pen - sive - ly roam.

an - der, twi - light_ is fad - ing, I pen - sive - ly_ roam.

MORE RHYTHM

Sometimes composers want music notes to move even faster. To show this when they write music, they add another beam to the group of notes, like this:

No beam	♩	say "ta"
One beam	♫	say "ti-ti"
Two beams	♬♬	say "ti-ri-ti-ri"

1. **mp**

ti-ri-ti-ri

2. **mf**

3. Key of F Major **f**

DO

4. Key of C Major **mp**

DO

5. Key of G Major **mp**

DO

6. Key of A Major **mf**

DO

EV'RY LITTLE BIT

1. Key of D Major

Audrey Snyder

Ev-'ry lit-tle smile, ev-'ry lit-tle friend-ship,

ev-'ry lit-tle laugh we share to-day, ev-'ry lit-tle hope,

ev-'ry lit-tle dream can help to chase the blues, chase them a-way.

2. Key of C Major

3. Key of E Major

INTERVALS

On the staff the *distance* from one note to another is called an *interval*. Intervals are measured by counting the lines and spaces from one note to the next. To find the number of the interval, begin on the first note and then count the lines and spaces until the next note is reached. For example:

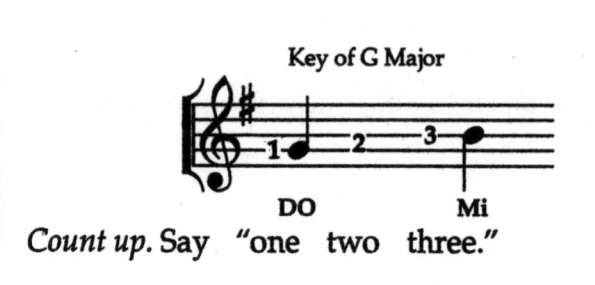

Key of G Major

Count up. Say "one two three."

These two notes are *three* lines and spaces apart, so in music this is called an interval of a *third*. All *skips* in music are intervals of a *third*.

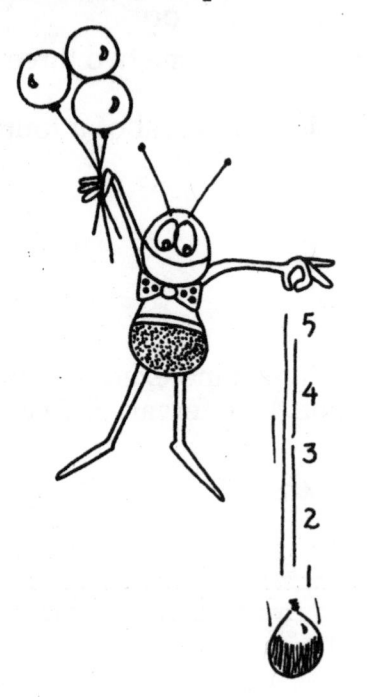

Here are some more examples:

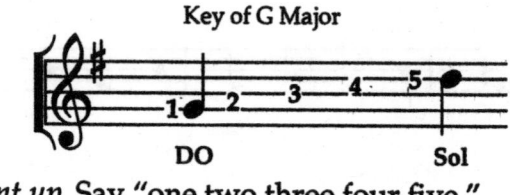

Key of G Major

Count up. Say "one two three four five."

This is an interval of a fifth. DO *up* to Sol is always an interval of a fifth.

Depending upon where the notes are on the staff, sometimes it is necessary to count *up* and sometimes it is necessary to count *down*.

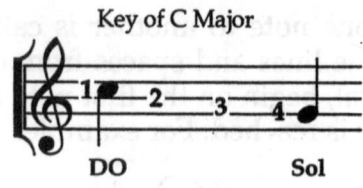

Key of C Major

DO   Sol

Count down.   Say "one two three four."

This is an interval of a fourth. DO *down* to Sol is always an interval of a fourth.

Here are some exercises using intervals of seconds, thirds, fourths, and fifths. Name the intervals and sing each exercise.

1. Key of G Major

DO

2. Key of B Major

Legato

DO

WHITE CORAL BELLS

3. Key of C Major

English

DO

JUMPING DO - FA - DO

DO *up* to FA is an interval of a FOURTH.

1. Key of F Major

DO *down* to FA is an interval of a FIFTH.

2. Key of C Major

3. Key of C Major

MORE RHYTHM

Sometimes composers beam notes together in combination. As you know, notes connected with two beams move faster than those connected with one beam.

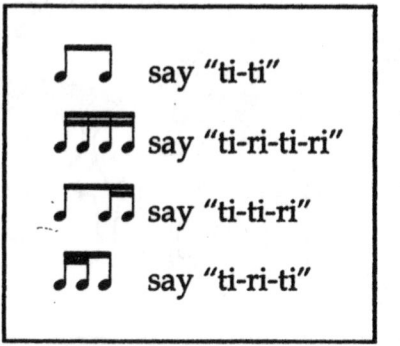

1.

2.

3.

4. Key of F Major

5. Key of D Major

REVIEW AND PRACTICE

1. Key of D Major

2. Key of C Major

3. Key of G Major

JUMPING RE - SOL - RE

RE *up* to SOL is an interval of a FOURTH.

1. Key of E Major

EQUESTRIAN MYSTERY TUNE EXCERPT

2. Key of F Major

RE *down* to SOL is an interval of a FIFTH.

3. Key of B Major

MARITAL MYSTERY TUNE EXCERPT

4. Key of B Major

REVIEW AND PRACTICE

1. Key of F Major

f

DO Re

2. Key of G Major

SKIP TO MY LOU

Folk Song

DO Mi *f*

Swing your part-ner   skip to my Lou,   swing your part-ner   skip   to my Lou,

swing your part - ner   skip   to my Lou,   skip   to my Lou, my   dar - ling.

3. Key of B Major

BRITISH MYSTERY TUNE

mf

DO Sol

4. Key of B Major

I

mf

rit. last time

mp

DO

II

mf

rit. last time

mp

DO Mi

5. Key of E Major

POLLY WOLLY DOODLE Excerpt

Folk Song

mf

DO

NATURAL MINOR
"LA" IS HOME BASE

As you know, when DO is the key center, the pattern DO Re Mi Fa Sol La Ti DO is called the Major Scale.

The same *pattern* is used to sing a *Natural Minor Scale*, but DO is no longer the key center. *LA becomes the key center.* When composers write music using the Natural Minor Scale, *LA is home base.*

Key of C Minor

LA Ti Do Re Mi Fa Sol LA

1. Key of G minor, LA is G.

mp

LA

HAUNTED HOUSE

2. Key of F minor

mf < *f*   > *pp*   < *f*   > *pp*

LA Do Mi

3. Key of F Minor

mf

I

LA

II

mf

LA

rit.

rit.

MID-WINTER

Audrey Snyder

1. Key of A Minor

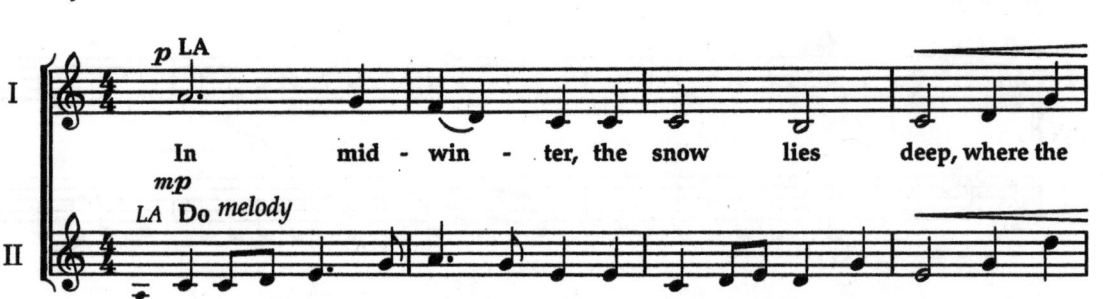

In mid - win - ter, the snow lies deep, where the

In the mid-win - ter, cold and bleak, a blan-ket of snow lies deep, where the

song can ne'er be___ heard, the world in si - lence sleeps.

song of a bird can ne'er be___ heard, the world in si - lence sleeps.

DONA NOBIS PACEM (Grant Us Peace)

Audrey Snyder

2. Key of C Minor

Do - na no - bis, Do - na no - bis,___

Do - na no - bis,___ Do - na no - bis,

___ Do - na no - bis pa - cem.

Do - na no - bis pa - cem.

REVIEW AND PRACTICE

1. Key of E Major

SING YOUR SONG

2. Key of C Major
Legato

Audrey Snyder

Congratulations on completing Volume I! You have mastered many of the skills necessary to become a self-sufficient sight-singer!